Greetings from Christmas Past

A MERRY CHRISTMAS TO YOU.

Greetings from

CHRISTMAS PAST

Bevis Hillier

The Herbert Press

To my two god-daughters, Rose Billington, & Ji Green.

© Copyright 1982
by The Herbert Press Limited
First published in Great Britain 1982 by
The Herbert Press Limited, 65 Belsize
Lane, London NW3 5AU

Designed by Gillian Greenwood
Printed and bound by South China
Printing Co., Hong Kong

UK ISBN 0 906969 23 9

Distributed in the USA by Universe
Books, 381 Park Avenue South, New
York, NY 10016
USA ISBN 0-87663-409-9

Acknowledgements

The cards illustrated are from the collections of David
Drummond's 'Pictures of Past Times' and the author, with the
exception of those on page 86 (top), kindly lent by Paul Anstee
of Bayly's Gallery, London, and pages 6, 23 (right), 41 (top), 59
(top), 72 (top), 83, 84 and 87 which are reproduced by courtesy
of The Victoria & Albert Museum.

Contents

The first Christmas card, 1843

Introduction

The Victorian Christmas card was a sophisticated folk art – a folk art of the Industrial Revolution. Like the slipware jugs and carved wooden love-spoons of earlier centuries, Victorian cards tell us a lot about the people who sent them. In fact, the removal of the element of hand-craftsmanship makes them *more* typical: the hand-made present represented only its maker; the mass-produced card was made with an eye on what the majority of 'consumers' were likely to want and to buy.

The first Christmas card was designed in 1843 by John Calcott Horsley, at the suggestion of Sir Henry Cole, a Victorian live-wire who was much involved in the Great Exhibition of 1851 and founded what is now the Victoria and Albert Museum. It was printed in lithography by Jobbins of Warwick Court, Holborn, London, and hand-coloured by a professional colourer named Mason. It was published at 'Felix Summerly's Home Treasury Office, 12 Old Bond Street, London' by Cole's friend Joseph Cundall. ('Felix Summerly' was the pseudonym under which Cole made 'art wares' in the new, more naturalistic style which he wanted to promote in place of sterile reliance on historicism, as in the Gothic revival.) Fewer than 1,000 copies of the card were sold, at 1s. each.

The card was divided into three panels, separated by the twiggy, leafing trelliswork acceptable to Felix Summerly principles. The central panel showed a family party in progress, with a toast being drunk: this led to inevitable protests by Victorian do-gooders that the card would encourage drunkenness, though as Gleeson White sarcastically asked in a special issue of *The Studio* in 1894, 'if we investigated all the cases of drunkenness in all these years, could we find a single one remotely traceable to this design of Mr Horsley's, or any of its fellows?' The side panels represent the spirit of Christmas charity: in one the poor are being fed, in the other, clothed. George Buday, whose *The History of the Christmas Card* (Rockliff, 1954) is the standard work, went to see Sir Henry Cole's granddaughter, who possessed a copy of the card sent to him by Horsley, with a heavily punning greeting based on the nursery rhyme 'Old King Cole', and the date 'Xmasse 1843'. The British Museum copy was also sent by Horsley and is dated 'Xmasse 1843'.

Cole's card was followed, in quick succession, by others privately printed. In 1845 the Revd Edward Bradley, who as 'Cuthbert Bede' wrote *The Adventures of Verdant Green* (1853), sent a Christmas card to his friends, lithographed by Lambert of Newcastle who in 1847 marketed the card for general sale. Thomas Sturrock and his friend Charles Drummond, of Leith, Scotland, designed a card of a laughing face with a Scottish New Year greeting, 'A Guid New Year an' Mony o' Them' at some time before 1846 (the precise date is not known). And William Maw Egley (1826-1916) designed a card in 1848, similar to Horsley's in the use of a rustic trellis and vine leaves to divide the composition, but with little figures are not unlike the 'fairy folk' of Dicky Doyle. Two original pencil sketches for the card, which was etched by Egley himself, are in the Victoria and Albert Museum.

Why, one might ask, was the Christmas card not invented much earlier? Why did periwigged Georgian squires not send pasteboard greetings to their friends? The custom of sending New Year gifts and tokens was of great antiquity. The ancient Egyptians had given small blue-glazed flasks with inscriptions about the approaching New Year. On the first day of January, the Romans exchanged greetings and presents, such as oil lamps decorated with a winged figure of Victory and the inscription: *Anno novo faustum felix tibi sit* (May the New Year be happy and lucky for you!). So why was the Christmas card delayed until the 1840s? The answer lies in the introduction of the Penny Post in 1840. Sir Rowland Hill's post office reform made it much easier to send greetings cards. Instead of the previous system, which charged 4*d.* within 15 miles, 5*d.* with 20 miles, 6*d.* within 30 miles, 7*d.* within 50 miles, 8*d.* within 80 miles and 1*s.* within 300 miles, with double rate if an envelope was used, the reform meant that letters were delivered to anywhere in Great Britain for 1*d.* For the first time, payment was in advance; the burden was no longer imposed on the recipient – such as poor Wordsworth, who once had to pay £7 for a batch of fan-mail.

Other circumstances also favoured the fledgling Christmas card. One was the development of colour printing by George Baxter and his followers. Another was the habit of affixing coloured commercial scraps to visiting cards and adding a Christmas greeting. But above all it was the makers of the already commercialized valentine cards who saw the rich potential of the Christmas card. Valentines were mainly confined to the young; and, except for confirmed Casanovas, one person usually sent one card. Christmas cards were for all age groups, and a person with fifty friends might well send fifty cards.

So it is not surprising that the early commercial Christmas cards had a strong family resemblance to contemporary valentines, down to the new machine-made paper 'lace' round the borders. It was claimed in a letter to *The Times* in 1883 that the first really ambitious commercial issue of Christmas cards was by Messrs Goodall, the playing-card manufacturers

Snowball card with paper 'lace' border

of Camden Town, in 1862. There were certainly publishers doing business on a smaller scale before that, among them several Baxter licensees, well known as chromolithographers, such as Kronheim (for whom Kate Greenaway was to draw her first designs while still a schoolgirl), Dickes and Mansell (p. 54, top left), or Leighton Brothers, whose director, G. C. Leighton, had learnt his craft from Baxter. But people who could remember most of the nineteenth century agreed that Goodall's was the first name to be prominently associated with Christmas card production. *The London Art Journal* of 1 December 1862 referred to 'An extensive series of cards, notepaper and envelopes of an exceedingly pure and beautiful character' produced by 'Messrs. Goodall & Son, card manufacturers of Camden Town, for Christmas and the New Year'. The paper added: 'They are in great variety – all being in "keeping" with the season; holly, ivy of course predominating in designs charmingly executed, and brilliantly coloured; and generally by excellent artists.' The second most prolific Christmas card maker of the early 1860s was probably Benjamin Sulman, of Upper Thames Street, London (later of City Road and Warwick Lane) who made small, beautifully engraved, embossed and die-stamped cards, often with 'lace' edges.

In 1867 Marcus Ward, a Belfast publisher, opened a London branch (Oriel House, Farringdon Street, designed by Walter Crane's brother Thomas, who became their design director). 'In the hands of this firm,' George Buday writes, 'Christmas card production ceased to be a sideline, but became instead a great and expanding industry . . .' Walter Crane naturally designed cards for them, and they were also to be a leading publisher of cards designed by Kate Greenaway, H. Stacy Marks and Moyr Smith, an 'Aesthetic movement' artist who also designed tiles for pottery firms. In 1882 *Punch* commented that 'Marcus Ward is to the front with his show, and *all* his Christmas *cards* are – trumps!' In 1897 the firm were awarded the Gold Medal of the Victorian Era Exhibition, Earl's Court, for their exhibit of lithography and stationery, 'embracing samples of their world-famed Christmas cards from 1867 to the present time'.

De La Rue was another publishing firm which added Christmas card production to a much wider repertoire of printing and paper-goods manufacture. In the 1820s, when its founder, Thomas De La Rue from Guernsey, was still in charge, it made embossed paper bonnets – perhaps the earliest recorded disposable paper clothing. It also printed playing cards and banknotes. It was Thomas De La Rue who discovered how to make the finest type of white, shiny-surfaced card, later adopted by many manufacturers for Christmas cards. Among their stable of artists were W. S. Coleman, well-known for his little nude girls, J. M. Dealy, another

As Time's Path
Beneath the Sun.

Bright be thine
this year begun.

Sepia design by Walter Crane

"For all" "Behold, I bring you good tidings of great joy which shall be to all people"

XMAS 1888.

Social Order

The New

With Walter Crane's Best Wishes

portrayer of fetching children, (see p. 85), and Ernest Griset, one of the most fanciful 'anthropomorphizers' of animals and birds.

Raphael Tuck, still prominent today among Christmas card manufacturers, began production about 1871, and pepped up the whole trade by holding competitions from 1880 with big prizes for Christmas card design. Royal Academicians judged the competitions, and the 925 designs submitted for the 1880 contest were exhibited in the Dudley Gallery. (The rising status of Christmas cards was also marked, at this time, by reviews of them, not unlike book reviews, in the national press.) Tuck gave away £500 in prizes in 1880 and bought a selection of designs for £2,500. The rewards were now so great that the best artists could make a living from Christmas card design. Kate Greenaway had received only about £3 for her first valentine, which sold more than 25,000 copies in a few weeks; but the *Windsor Magazine* recorded in 1897 that the fee for the average design was three guineas, and an outstanding designer could make as much as £900 a year. By this stage, Royal Academicians did not scorn to provide Christmas card designs. Raphael Tuck published some by Marcus Stone RA in 1882. Other Academicians who designed for Tuck were G. H. Boughton, W. C. T. Dobson, J. C. Herbert, G. D. Leslie, H. S. Marks, E. J. Poynter, J. Sant and W. F. Yeames, painter of 'And When Did You Last See Your Father?'. *Punch* commented: 'This comes of having been Christened RAPHAEL, which must be at once suggestive of the highest Art.'

In 1893 Queen Victoria granted Tuck a royal warrant. *Home Chat* recorded of the Queen in 1895: 'Not only does she procure at great expense cards for all her royal relatives – and we know how numerous they are – but she buys not less than thousands to send to her neighbours at Windsor and Osborne.' Her main choice for 1895 was of children dancing in period costume; but she also ordered nearly 100 of a card which, said *Home Chat*, 'may be said to have reached the culminating point in Christmas cards. Standing up properly, it occupies a space of 12 inches high by 10 inches wide and 8 deep . . . It represents the offering by the Wise Men of the East of gifts to the infant Saviour . . . The whole is got up in a most lavish manner and leaves the beholder in wonder as to how the Christmas card of the present day can be improved upon.' The same article also recorded that a large number of Christmas cards had been ordered by Mrs Cleveland, wife of the President of the United States. 'The designs are peculiarly interesting, inasmuch as they are all of more or less Puritan nature or time, and are unequalled for chaste simplicity and good taste. Thousands of Americans will be the proud recipients of these cards this Christmas time from their President and his wife.'

Nymphet by W. S. Coleman

By that time, there was a flourishing American Christmas card industry. The first American Christmas card seems to have been issued by R. H. Pease of New York at some time between 1850 and 1852. When George Buday's book was at page proof stage, in the early 1950s, he was sent, by Mr E. D. Chase, a reproduction of this card, of which the only known copy was in the possession of the Rust Craft Company. No date appeared on the lithograph, but by careful research Mr Chase had established that it must have been produced between 1850 and 1852, since it was only during those years that Pease occupied the building which was pictured prominently on the card. Buday gives this description of the card:

> Above the holly-decorated curved display line, carrying Pease's advertisement ['Pease's Great Varety (*sic*) Store in the Temple of Fancy'], the design includes the features of a small, raeher elf-like Santa Claus with fur-trimmed cap, sleigh and reindeer. A ball-room with dancers, the building marked 'Temple of Fancy', an array of Christmas presents and Christmas dishes and drinks decorate the four corners of the card, while in the centre we see a young couple with three children visibly delighted with their presents; behind the family group a black servant is laying the table for the Christmas dinner. In addition to the central 'A Merry Christmas and A Happy New Year' the ornamented lettering includes 'To:' and 'From:' with spaces to be filled by the sender.

But this appears to have been a 'one-off', and the publisher regarded as 'the Father of the American Christmas Card' is Louis Prang, whose plant was in Roxbury, a suburb of Boston. He had arrived in New York from Germany in April 1850, after the failure of the 1848 Revolutions in Europe. He was an idealist with boundless confidence in the New World; and in America is remembered for the 'Prang method of education' which he devised, as well as for his Christmas cards. After working as a wood-engraver at *Gleason's Pictorial,* he set up as a lithographer with Joseph Mayer in Boston (1856) but in 1860 the partnership was dissolved and L. Prang & Co. was established. Prang invented a system of colour-printing from zinc plates, instead of from the lithographic stone. 'I have used zinc plates for nearly all my color plates since 1873,' he told the Chicago *Lithographer and Printer* in 1884, 'and am positive that I have saved thereby fifty thousand dollars.' Alongside his undoubted business acumen, there was a genuine idealistic desire to bring good art to the masses. It was he who instituted the idea of competitions for Christmas card designs in 1880 – an idea instantly copied by his rivals in England and Germany, Tuck, Hildesheimer & Faulkner and S. Hildesheimer. The first prize was $1,000 and Louis Comfort Tiffany was among the judges. Prang had raised the stakes, and the English manufacturers who were unwilling or unable to join in this high-pressure competition abandoned

A card by Louis Prang

A card by S. Hildesheimer & Co.

Christmas card production – De La Rue after only ten years of production, in 1885; Marcus Ward about 1895.

Prang's cards are noted for their flawless register. At first, from 1875 to 1879, the main production was of small, single cards (3½ x 2in. or 4 x 2½in.) printed on one side only, often with flowers, fruit or birds. Black-background cards were also popular. By the late 1870s, Prang's cards were becoming more elongated (5½ x 2¾in. and 6¾ x 2¼in.) and large cards came in during the 1880s (6 x 8in.; 7 x 10in.). Prang, like Ward and De La Rue in England, despised trick cards or cards cluttered up with lacy or tinsel decorations. Artists who worked for Prang included O. E. Whitney (designer of some of the early, floral cards), Rosina Emmett (winner of the First Prize in 1880), Elihu Vedder (winner of the First Prize in 1881), Will H. Low, Thomas Moran and Henry Sandham. In 'A Brief History of the Christmas Card' in the *New Haven Colony Historical Society Journal* (vol. 9, September–December 1960), Mr Carroll Alton Means recorded that Prang also commissioned Civil War scenes by Winslow Homer. He also states that 'Prang's business flourished until 1895 when there was very stiff competition from Germany.'

Germany was not only a land of factories in the mid nineteenth century, it was also fashionable in England, through royal connexions, and was naturally popular among the large German immigrant community in America. Queen Victoria's immediate ancestry was German, and her consort was German by birth. The Victorian house contained Berlin woolwork, German pianos, German magic lanterns, German toys and Grimm and *Struwwelpeter* for the nursery. The custom of the Christmas tree came over with Prince Albert (see p. 23). The Pre-Raphaelites were strongly influenced by a group of German artists, the Nazarenes. China souvenirs bearing transfer-printed views of Margate or Leamington Spa were 'Made in Germany'.

It was natural for the Germans, with their great printing and engraving traditions (Gutenberg, Dürer and the rest) to cash in on the demand for well-designed and well-printed cards. S. Hildesheimer & Co. were at Silk Street, London, from 1876, with branches in Manchester and New York. In 1879 they introduced a set of cards called the 'Penny Basket'. It was at this time that Christmas cards ceased to be sold merely by booksellers and stationery shops. Now they were on sale in toy-shops and tobacconists as well, and drapery stores also began to enter the competition, the first to do so being Bollen and Tidswell, who placed single orders of £10,000 for cards.

S. Hildesheimer also reproduced etchings and water-colours by Wilfrid Ball, a member of the Royal Society of Painter-Etchers. These

A card designed by Helena Maguire for W. Hagelberg

were mounted in the form of a miniature sketch book: in 1884 six such booklets were published, covering such beauty spots as Burnham Beeches, Epping Forest, Windsor and Putney (still a beauty spot in 1884!). Accompanying the etchings were facsimile hand-written notes – for example (of Putney): 'Mr Whistler, the finest living etcher, was the first to show us the picturesque quaintness of Old Putney Bridge, now so soon to be demolished.'

S. Hildesheimer held a Christmas card competition and exhibition at St James's Hall, London, in 1881, in direct imitation of Prang's first competition. The firm of Hildesheimer & Faulkner, in Jewin Street, London, from 1877, arranged a big competition and exhibition in 1882. The exhibition was held in the Suffolk Street Gallery, later the Royal Society of British Artists' Gallery, and they paid out £5,000 in prizes. Miss Alice Havers, who won the first prize of £250, was the daughter of the manager of the Falkland Islands and married the artist Frederick Morgan. Through her success in the competition, she became one of the most sought-after artists, and continued designing cards up to her death in 1890. The art critic of *Society* thus described her prize-winning entry, 'A Dream of Patience':

> An idyll set in a forest with groups, painted with Leightonesque finesse, of lovely female forms; the backs of the cards, cloud studies worthy of Turner, of early dawn and the setting sun, and cumulo-cirro banks, silver-lined by a half-hidden moon – this seems to me the gem of the collection.

Hildesheimer & Faulkner, which still flourishes as C. W. Faulkner & Co., introduced photogravure cards in 1892; their other technical innovations included mixing silver with the colours so that 'in winter scenes the glistening of the snow may be more faithfully rendered'. Another leading German publisher of cards was Wolff Hagelberg of Berlin, who seems to have had some connexion with S. Hildesheimer. Hagelberg's London representative in the early 1860s was A. Angermann; after 1869, E. Falck. His London branch was at 12 Bunhill Row and he also had a New York Office at 36 and 38 East 12th Street from 1889. Hagelberg's cards were often of guardian angels watching over children. He also made novelty cards to commemorate the Colonial Exhibition at South Kensington in 1886, and another with a Punch and Judy show revealed in silhouette when the card was held up to the light. Other German publishers included Bernhard Ollendorff of Berlin (see p. 54), the Obpacher Brothers of Munich, and the successful Lothar Meggendorfer of Munich, whose trick cards sold well in London and America from the 1870s to the 1890s.

By the 1890s, German imports of all kinds had ceased to be fashionable and had become a commercial enemy to be attacked. In 1896 – just about the time that Prang in America and Marcus Ward in England were driven out of production by German competition – E. E. Williams wrote his book *Made in Germany*, which contained this passage:

> Roam the house over, and the fateful mark will greet you at every turn, from the piano in your drawing room to the mug on your kitchen dresser, blazoned though it be with the legend *A Present from Margate*. Descend to your domestic depths, and you shall find your very drainpipes German made. You pick out of the grate the paper wrappings from a book consignment, and they are also 'Made in Germany'. You stuff them into the fire, and reflect that the poker in your hand was forged in Germany. As you rise from your hearthrug you knock over an ornament on your mantelpiece; picking up the pieces you read, on the bit that formed the base, 'Manufactured in Germany'. And you jot your dismal reflections down with a pencil that was made in Germany. At midnight, your wife comes home from an opera which was made in Germany, has been here enacted by singers and conductor and players made in Germany. You go to bed, and glare wrathfully at a text on the wall; it is illuminated with an English village church, and it was 'Printed in Germany'. If you are imaginative and dyspeptic, you drop off to sleep only to dream that St. Peter (with a duly stamped halo round his head and a bunch of keys from the Rhineland) has refused you admission into Paradise, because you bear not the mark of the Beast upon your forehead, and are not of German make. But you console yourself with the thought that it was only a Bierhaus Paradise anyway; and you are awakened by the sonorous brass of a German band.

If he had thought of them, Williams would certainly have included German-made Christmas cards in his litany of hate. The period at which he was writing is about the last in which Christmas cards of interest to the collector were being made. The last four pages of this book clearly show the decline which set in after Victoria's death in 1901 – either through the blowsy excesses of late and debased Art Nouveau or through shoddiness of production and the use of picture postcards.

It is perhaps an exaggeration to call Victorian Christmas cards 'a microcosm of the age'. Too many of them are on religious themes; too many are simply pretty pictures. But even the religious cards (which, incidentally, are among the most decorative – see pages 48-51) give an indication of Victorian religiosity; and even the choice of scenes unrelated to religion or to Christmas gives us an idea of Victorian taste. The sadistic cards – in which geese are being pelted by oranges or distraught elves captured in a shrimping net – show the streak of unusual cruelty in Victorian England, which was perhaps a concomitant of sexual repression. (The suggestive nude nymphets of W. S. Coleman, much admired by Ruskin, and of Miss E. G. Thomson, much admired by Lewis Carroll, may have had a similar origin.)

The instances where politics enter Christmas cards are rare. Walter Crane designed a card in 1874 in which Lord Derby is being replaced by Father Christmas as popular favourite; 'Triumphant Return of Mr Christmas' shows him standing in an open carriage with, as coat of arms, a plum pudding, knife and fork. Alfred Bryan, who worked for Hildesheimer and Faulkner, specialized in political cartoon cards, of Gladstone in an express train ('I shall soon be back into power') or Lord Randolph Churchill, Winston's father, sitting on a crescent moon and playing a mandoline. These were jocular and uncontentious; but the 'Ode to the Specials' which appeared on an Angus Thomas card at Christmas 1887, after demonstrations in Trafalgar Square that year, would certainly have been offensive to the crowd who fought the police on 'Bloody Sunday' (13 November 1887) and to relatives of the two people killed by the 'Specials' on that occasion.

The Irish MP William O'Brien, who was in prison for organizing riots against Irish landlords, had refused to wear jail clothes and had wrung special privileges for political prisoners. 'Bloody Sunday' was a demonstration over his case. The Commissioner of Police, Sir Charles Warren, was anxious to put an end to open-air meetings in Trafalgar Square. He had been alternately permitting and banning them. The meeting of 13 November was summoned in defiance of a prohibition and its aim, 'to demand the release of William O'Brien, MP', was chosen so as to attract Irish as well as Radical militants. The radicals were led by two MPs, R.

Cunninghame Graham and John Burns, who were arrested and subsequently sent to prison for six weeks. The police fought hard and long against superior numbers until Foot Guards and Life Guards arrived and cleared the square. No shot was fired and the Riot Act was not read. There were over 100 casualties and two of the crowd died of their injuries. Sir Robert Ensor, who describes the event as 'the most considerable *émeute* in London during the latter half of the nineteenth century', adds: 'Bitter memories of it lasted in the working-class districts for over twenty years. Much odium fell on Warren, who was indeed largely to blame.' (Sir Robert Ensor, *England, 1870-1914*, Oxford, 1968 edn. p. 181.)

But Angus Thomas, in their Christmas cards referring to the tragedy (hardly a subject to foster peace and goodwill to all men), took the side of the Establishment, with a picture of a truncheon ('To be used with great care: for external application only') and the following verse;

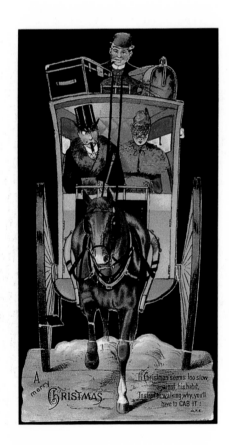

A merry CHRISTMAS. If Christmas seems too slow, against his habit, Instead of walking why, you'll have to CAB IT!

ODE TO THE 'SPECIALS'
In Trafalgar Bay where the Frenchmen lay,
    A Hero was Nelson there!
But nothing was he tho' King of the Sea,
    To the Kings of Trafalgar Square!
With Jack on the watch and with *battened* hatch,
    There France in its pride was quashed,
Washed in the wave where they found a grave –
    But they *baton'd* 'The Great Unwashed'!
Then surely the fame of Nelson's name
    The 'Specials' have right to share:
'*He* won the day in Trafalgar Bay,
    But *They* (?) in Trafalgar Square!'

A more radical Christmas-card sentiment is found on a card published in Richmond, Virginia, in the 1860s:

Anathema on him who screws and hoards,
    Who robs the poor of wheat, potatoes, bread;
On all his gains may withering blights descend –
    On body, bones, on intellect and head.

In 1918, the last year of the Great War, the Campbell Art Company, USA, published an amusing 'Hooverized Christmas Greeting', drawing attention to President Hoover's economy drive and the current 'hard times' by a deliberately cheap-looking card with 'rationed' holly and mistletoe sprigs and 'camouflaged ribbon' (ordinary string), with this verse:

I've Hooverized on Pork and beans
    And Butter, Cake and Bread,
I've cut out Auto-riding
    And now I walk instead;

Poor children were sentimentalized

I've Hooverized on sugar,
 On Coal and Light and Lard,
And here's my Xmas Greeting
 On a Hoover Christmas Card.

'I wish you a very M.C. and H.N.Y.'

For those who prefer the trappings of history (transport, for example) to history itself, there is plenty of interest in Christmas cards. The stage-coach battling through a blizzard (with or without glitter-dust) is a cliché of the more conventional modern card. Today, coaching is not even a memory; in the 1880s it was still a reality. But new-fangled bicycles also appear on several cards; and Buday refers to one 'charmingly naïve card' which shows 'a boy, representing the New Year, riding a steam engine with a fully decorated Christmas tree behind him'. (Buday, *op. cit.,* p. 131.) Decorative ships were also popular, perhaps with seasonal thoughts of 'I Saw Three Ships Come Sailing By', but no such pretty sentiment was behind the card of 1917, sent out by the Dover Patrol, which showed the German battle-cruiser *Tirpitz* approaching a floating object on which the word MINE is visible just above the water. In the 1890s, the 'new monstrosity from France', the automobile or motor car, became a motif for cards. Sir Frank Lockwood, the judge-cum-cartoonist, sketched one as his personal Christmas card for 1897; and in 1903 Professor Hubert Herkomer, the painter, sent a card of a motor car travelling at full speed. (This card is now in the Victoria and Albert Museum.) Motor cars were still novel enough by the later Edwardian period to be used on postcards with Christmas greetings (see p. 95).

Of the harsher realities of Victorian social life we inevitably get little impression from Christmas cards, for as Buday points out in a moving passage, the tribulations of the poor were sentimentalized and made picturesque for public consumption:

Very characteristically, children of the poor were frequently the subjects of Christmas cards. Their living conditions and miserable childhood was beginning to be felt by many to be a disgrace to society in the second half of the Victorian era. Correspondingly, a sentimental aura is drawn around these poor, hard-working and much-exploited children, to whom ice and snow were no mere fun, but the cause of harder living and additional work. The artists usually painted them on Christmas cards with the sympathy due to little ragged crossing-sweepers, tattered torchbearers or newspaper boys, though seldom with the force of social criticism. This attitude seemed natural enough in view of their public, and if they were the incentive to a larger tip or a hot meal, so much the better. They were not aiming to reform the social evils of the day; they were to supersede them for the duration of Christmas. (Buday, *op.cit.,* p. 137.)

A Happy Christmas

Robins were among the most common motifs

Christmas cards have been collected since the nineteenth century – not only by their recipients, who pasted them into scrap-books, but by learned connoisseurs who researched into the history of the firms which produced them. The greatest Christmas card collector of all time was Jonathan King who, in addition to trying to buy samples of every card published in his day, even bought up some of the manufacturing companies in the later nineteenth century. His accumulation of cards reached such huge proportions that he turned his houses in Islington into a museum of Christmas cards. In the 1890s the collection weighed between six and seven tons, and included about 163,000 varieties of cards published between 1862 and 1895, but mainly after 1880. He grouped his cards according to subject: one of his contemporaries recalled being shown 'ten volumes of robin Christmas cards', 'a volume of snowmen', another of insects, another of donkeys and so on in endless array. Just as misers, like Silas Marner, are punished in stories by having their hoards stolen, so poor King received poetic justice for his obsessional amassing of Christmas cards: nearly all of them were destroyed in a fire in 1918. That must have removed many unique cards from the market for ever; but there are still enough left to keep hundreds of collectors busy for the rest of their lives. I bought the cards illustrated in this book (except for those lent by the Victoria and Albert Museum, David Drummond's 'Pictures of Past Times' and Paul Anstee) in three shops only – two in London, one in Oxford – over a period of four years. The average price was £5; the most expensive was the Kate Greenaway card on page 82 at £20.

There are so many different ways of collecting. You can collect particular publishers, such as Raphael Tuck, or particular artists, such as H. Stacy Marks. A very amusing collection could be made of the maudlin and mawkish 'sentiment writers' whose work often appears on the backs of cards, including Helen Marion Burnside, the 'Poet Laureate of Christmas Cards' (see pp. 36, 54 and 92), or the indefatigable Major Samuel Cowan, MA (see pp. 44 and 60). This masterpiece is from an 1884 card which shows stars over a desolate lake;

There arose a joyful clamour from the wildfowl of the mere
Beneath the stars across the snow like clear bells ringing,
And a voice within cried: 'Listen! Christmas carols even here!
Though they be dumb yet o'er their work the stars and snow are singing.'

You can collect as Jonathan King did, by subject: George Buday devotes a whole chapter to robin redbreast cards, and discusses the legends associated with the favourite bird. One of them suggests that the robin's breast became red when, trying to ease Christ's suffering on His way to the Crucifixion, a robin pulled out a thorn from the crown of thorns, and in so doing a drop of His blood fell on its chest and has remained there ever since. And, wondering why the robin should have been thought so specially appropriate at Christmas time, Buday recalls that the custom of hunting a robin, as a kind of sacrificial substitute for the red of human blood, originally took place on December 24, and later on the 26th, St Stephen's Day. Jonathan King's visitor, a reporter from the Islington *Daily Gazette,* was amazed to see 'ten volumes of robins, revealing robins red in all imaginable styles – comic robins, perky robins, robins in the snow'. The subject headings in this book will suggest some other themes for the collector – among them, flowers, dogs, cats, children, dolls, toys and the festivities of Christmas themselves. A really masochistic collector might like to make a collection of today's Christmas cards. I analysed a selection of these in *Punch,* 30 November 1977. They included a 'flicker' Christmas card in which Santa Claus does a pirouette and then parts his robes for a quick 'flash'. Will that tell future generations something about the mores of our time?

With all the Frills

A MERRY CHRISTMAS

A MERRY CHRISTMAS
AND A HAPPY NEW YEAR

In the 1860s and 1870s the most common kind of Christmas card was the small chromolithograph with a paper 'lace' border. These were closely related to the contemporary valentine cards. Some were English, but many were printed in Germany. Few were marked with the publishers' names.

The design of the comic card (right) anticipates by a century the 'ball wheelbarrow' invented by a student at the Royal College of Art, London, in the 1960s, and is one of many Christmas cards portraying clowns (see pp. 42-3). The close family link with valentines is emphasized by the card which shows a boy and girl in party clothes with a greeting to a 'dear and loving friend'. Two of the cards show girls wearing muffs, very fashionable in the 1870s. In Victorian times the word 'muff' was often used also to signify a duffer. Today both the garment and the slang usage are virtually extinct.

WELCOME UNTO THEE,
A HAPPY CHRISTMAS, TO YOU AND ME

A HAPPY NEW YEAR

A Christmas Greeting Now I send

To You My Dear & Loving Friend

A Merry Christmas and a Happy New Year.

THE COMPLIMENTS OF THE SEASON.

BRANDY SNAPS

Cards decorated with tiny but finely
detailed photographs still had an
appealing novelty in the early days
of photography. In these 1860s
examples the subjects are the tradi-
tional Christmas dinner and a
country lass gathering Yule fuel. She
looks like a miniature version of one
of the studies of servant girls by Mrs
Julia Margaret Cameron, one of the
Old Masters of photography. This
type of card is closely related to
books of the same period illustrated
with 'tipped-in' photographs. An
edition of Gray's poems often given
as a prize at Eton was decorated in
this way; and a number of travel
books appeared with photographic
illustrations by the intrepid authors.

The Christmas dinner scene is a
delightful vignette of mid-Victorian
society: the paterfamilias, or perhaps
a bachelor uncle who is (in more than
one sense) 'a bit of a card' is making a
speech in the characteristically cluttered interior. The ladies have flowers
in their hair, but no funny hats.

The
FESTIVE TREE

The Christmas tree was a German institution. In Luther's time, in the sixteenth century, Christmas trees were decorated with lights, though at first gifts were placed round them, not hung from the branches.

Prince Albert introduced the custom into England, setting up a tree at Windsor Castle in 1841. Victorian trees were hung with lanterns, and often with fragile, silvered glass ornaments made on the same principle as electric light bulbs. From the tree, children took the prizes they won in party games (see pp. 39-41).

The hand-coloured semi-photographic card (right) was published by Davidson Brothers of Manchester and London (1880s-90s). In 1894 Gleeson White, Editor of *The Studio*, praised their 'excellent taste . . . full of dainty inventions'. It is interesting to note that miniature flags form part of the tree's decoration. *The Home Book* (Frederick Warne, 1867) contained engravings of the chief flags of the world, 'beginning with the glorious banner of St George'. The nations represented were England, France, America, Austria, Prussia, Russia, Italy, Portugal, Spain and Turkey. The same book gave instructions for gilding walnuts for the tree and for covering green twigs with crystals by immersing them in alum solution.

The ceremony of decorating the tree, one of the most enjoyable Christmas institutions, is delightfully evoked by D. H. Lawrence in his novel *Aaron's Rod* (1922):

O'er you may Heaven's blessing dwell,
At Christmas and all times as well!
DAVIDSON BROTHERS   COPYRIGHT

The two children were squatted on the floor by the tree. They had a wooden box from which they had taken many little newspaper packets which they were spreading out like wares . . .

Millicent was saying: 'Now I'll undo the first, and you shall have the second. I'll take this—'

She unwrapped the bit of newspaper and disclosed a silvery ornament for a Christmas tree: a frail thing like a silver plum, with deep rosy indentations on each side.

'Oh!' she exclaimed. 'Isn't it lovely!'

Her fingers cautiously held the long bubble of silver and glowing rose, cleaving to it with a curious, irritating possession. The man's eyes moved away from her. The lesser child was fumbling with one of the little packets.

'Oh!'—a wail went up from Millicent—'You've taken one!—you didn't wait.'. . .

At length Marjory had got out her treasure—a little silvery bell, with a glass drop hanging inside. The bell was made of frail glassy substance, light as air.

'Oh, the bell!' rang out Millicent's clanging voice. 'The bell! It's my bell. My bell! It's mine! Don't break it, Marjory. Don't break it, will you?'. . .

Millicent began with hasty, itching fingers to unclose another package.

'Aw—aw, mother, my peacock—aw, my peacock, my green peacock!' Lavishly she hovered over a sinuous greenish bird, with wings and tail of spun glass, pearly, and body of deep electric green.

'It's mine—my green peacock! It's mine, because Marjory's had one wing off, and mine hadn't. My green peacock that I love? I love it!'

Evergreen Traditions

*When rosemary and bays, the
          Poet's crown,
Are bawl'd, in frequent cries,
          through all the town,
Then judge the festival of
          Christmas near,
Christmas, the joyous period of the
          year.
Now with bright holly all your
          temples strow,
With lawrel green, and sacred
          mistletoe.*

Trivia John Gay (1716)

Christmas is celebrated on the same date as a festival much older than Christ. Like Easter (named after the pagan goddess Eostre), it had heathen antecedents. According to the Venerable Bede, the heathen year began on December 25; the last month of the Old Year and the first month of the New Year were both included in the portmanteau name Giuli, the modern Yule.

In the Roman festival of the January Kalends, a few days after the Saturnalia, the houses were decorated with lights and greenery. Although the Christian church condemned Kalends decorations – as late as the sixth century the *capitula* of Bishop Martin of Braga forbade the adorning of houses with laurels and green trees – the custom found its way even into churches. As far back as the fifteenth century, according to Stow's *Survey of London*, it was the custom at Christmas for 'every man's house, as also the parish churches' to be 'decked with holm ivy, bays and whatsoever the season of the year afforded to be green. The conduits and standards in the streets were

My best wishes for Christmas.

likewise garnished.' And writing in 1913, Clement Miles in his *Christmas in Ritual and Tradition, Christian and Pagan*, recorded that 'Many people of the last generation will remember the old English mode of decoration – how sprigs of holly and yew, stuck into holes in the high pews, used to make the churches into miniature forests.'

Only upon the mistletoe was there an ecclesiastical taboo (though it is represented on a tomb of the Berkeleys in Bristol Cathedral). This parasitic shrub was famous in pagan legend for causing the death of Balder, the Norse god of light, who was stabbed to death by a dart of mistletoe; and Pliny, writing in the first century AD, gave an account of the use of mistletoe in Druidic ceremonies. Beneath its sinister, pallid berries, Victorian prudery could be temporarily waived: kissing under the mistletoe was an exclusively English custom (presumably because Continentals kiss each other all the time, mistletoe or no mistletoe). Before the introduction of commercial paper-chains, festoons of holly and ivy decorated middle-class drawing rooms. On Twelfth Night, all decorations had to come down to avoid bad luck – a custom which survives.

WISHING YOU A MERRY CHRISTMAS.

WISHING YOU A MERRY CHRISTMAS

WITH THE YEAR'S BLESSING IN ATTENDANCE.

See, Amid the Winter Snow

Victorians, too, seem to have dreamed of a White Christmas – and it was a dream that often came true. Out came the sledges and ice-skates; snowmen were constructed with coals for eyes; church lights glimmered welcomingly across the wintry fields.

The Cold War of snowballing was mercilessly waged, with little discrimination about targets; the elderly were fair game. The Raphael Tuck card which shows a boy about to pelt an old couple has this rhyme on the back, by Frederick Langbridge:

A peaceful unsuspecting pair
* Who saunter forth to take the air –*
His hat with wide and curly brim,
* Her fat round cheek half turned to*
*   him,*
And ready furnished, free to all,
* Material good for shot and ball –*
Could mortal boy the chance have
*   missed*
* To knead a bombshell in his fist,*
Take aim, and watch with joy
*   o'erflowed,*
* The missile strike and straight*
*   explode?*

The Yule log, seen on one of these cards being dragged home on a set of wheels, is no longer an essential part of the Christmas festivities for most of us; it was already declining in significance by 1913 when Clement Miles's *Christmas in Ritual and Tradition, Christian and Pagan* was published, but Miles commented that 'within the memory of many it was a very essential element in the celebration of the festival, not merely as giving out welcome warmth in the midwinter cold, but as possessing

WITH EVERY BEST WISH OF THE SEASON WE GREET THEE.

BRINGING HOME THE YULE-LOG.

WHILE CHRISTMAS IS HERE, BE ALL OF GOOD CHEER.

Prize Design.   Nº 377 Copyright.

occult, magical properties.' And Miles believed that 'In some remote corners of England it probably lingers yet.'

The Yule log, which actually bore the name of the pagan festival, and certainly had a pagan significance, was part of the Christmas festivities in many parts of Europe, especially Scandinavia. As practised in England, the custom was celebrated in these lines of Robert Herrick:

> Come, bring with a noise,
>   My merry, merry boys,
> The Christmas Log to the firing:
>   While my good Dame she
>   Bids ye all be free,
> And drink to your hearts' desiring.
>   With the last year's Brand
>   Light the new Block, and
> For good success in his spending,
>   On your psaltries play,
>   That sweet luck may
> Come while the log is a-teending.*

From these lines, Miles speculates that 'the lighting of the log at Christmas is a shrunken remnant of the keeping up of a perpetual fire, the continuity being to some extent preserved by the use of a brand from last year's blaze.' This theory was bolstered by Sir Lawrence Gomme, who wrote in his *Folk Lore Relics of Early Village Life* (1883) that 'From there being an ever-burning fire, it has come to be that the fire must not be allowed to be extinguished on the last day of the old year, so that the old year's fire may last into the new year.' Like the evergreen decorations, the Yule log reassuringly emphasized the continuity of life in a grim, uncertain world.

*kindling

Compliments of the Season.

A MERRY CHRISTMAS — ACCORDING AS IT FALLS.

May your Christmas joys each year increase!

With all good Christmas wishes

*A mirthful
merry time, this Christmas*

T.H.LCESHEIMER AND CO LIMITED   N°1269 COPYRIGHT   PRINTED IN GERMANY

No common palette, brush or paint, | But here's the best my hand can do—
Can shadow forth the children's saint, | May Santa Claus be kind to you!

W. HAGELBERG.   N°460. BERLIN.

Olde Worlde

Christmas was a time for looking back and savouring the traditions of Olde England. These two cards represent the two main kinds of historical nostalgia in Victorian England. One was for the early seventeenth century, also exemplified by Walter Thornbury's book of poems *Songs of the Cavaliers and Roundheads* (1857), illustrated by Henry Stacy Marks, well-known as a designer of Christmas cards; and by paintings such as 'And When Did You Last See Your Father' by W. F. Yeames, another leading designer of Christmas cards. The other strand of nostalgia was for medieval England, as portrayed in the poetry of Tennyson and the Pre-Raphaelites' paintings of Blessèd Damosels and Very Parfit Gentil Knights. Food always seemed to be an important ingredient of such cards: it was the roast beef of Old England (and the boars' heads, larks' tongue pies, capons and bowls of wassail) that people liked to remember at Christmas, not the more spiritual and ascetic side, of vigils before tombs or penitential pilgrimages. With no welfare system to rescue them, poverty was what the Victorians dreaded: 'Christmas Day in the Workhouse' was the salutary recitation piece most favoured at parties. The nostalgic Christmas cards reassuringly showed England as a cornucopia of good things.

Tally Ho!

A CHRISTMAS GREETING.

A HAPPY CHRISTMASTIDE

A MERRY CHRISTMAS TO YOU.

ALL HAPPINESS IS LARGELY DEPENDENT ON OURSELVES.

In the early days of Christmas cards, they were sent mainly by the upper and upper-middle classes – huntin', shootin' and fishin' folk who might have a town house but who would probably spend the Christmas holiday in their country homes. So hunting scenes and jokes about bumpkins often appear. The card of the lady rider was issued by De La Rue & Co. of London, best known today as printers of banknotes. That of the yokels carrying geese (with the somewhat materialist legend) is dated 1879.

SUMMER IS ICUMEN

A HAPPY CHRISTMAS

But some Christmas cards also looked forward – to the spring and summer to come. (Today this tradition is continued – not in Christmas cards, but in the articles on summer holidays which appear in the newspapers in January.)

To Victorians who survived into the middle of the twentieth century, the summers of their childhood seemed in memory longer and hotter than any they had known as their blood thinned. English fiction is full of these wistful, sun-dappled retrospects, such as that of Arnold Bennett's *Anna of the Five Towns*, who first appears as 'A little girl of twelve years, dressed in a cream-coloured frock, with a wide and heavy straw hat' – like a girl in one of these cards – and enjoys a memorable school-treat picnic:

MAY YOU SPEND A HAPPY CHRISTMAS

The sun shone generously on scores of vivid and frail toilettes, and parasols made slowly-moving hemispheres of glowing colour against the rich green of the grass. All around were yellow cornfields, and meadows where cows of a burnished brown indolently meditated upon the phenomena of a school-treat. Every hedge and ditch and gate and stile was in that ideal condition of plenary correctness . . . The sky, of an intense blue, was a sea in which large white clouds sailed gently, but capriciously . . .

MAY MERRY JOYS ATTEND YOUR CHRISTMASTIDE
AND HAPPINESS THROUGHT ALL YOUR NEW YEAR GLIDE

A Bright and Happy New Year.

33

Stocking Up

The children hung up their stockings (pillowcases for the affluent) for Santa Claus to fill. A rather unorthodox variation on the old myth is shown in the card above, which bears this rhyme:

Hang stockings high,
Christmas is nigh,
And birds will surely find them;
And when they go
They will, I know,
Leave many gifts behind them.

Is this a piece of malicious irony, belonging to Victorian sadism along with Struwwelpeter and Cruel Frederick? The birds do not look big enough to bring anything very substantial.

Welcome old Father Christmas,
With all his fun and festive cheer.

With best wishes of the Season.

Hello, Dolly

For the girls, there were dolls and dolls' houses.

S. Hildesheimer & Co. issued the 'fathers and mothers' card; Hildesheimer & Faulkner produced that of the girl hanging out dolly's undies. (This card is inscribed on the back: 'With Katie's love to Gertie. Xmas 1886'.) The dolls' house card was designed at Raphael Tuck's studios in England and printed at the 'fine art works' in Nuremberg, Bavaria. The verse is by the ineffable Helen Marion Burnside (b. 1843), the 'Poet Laureate of Christmas Cards', who is said to have written some 6,000 Christmas card 'sentiments' for American and British publishers between 1874 and 1900.

TOYS FOR BOYS

A JOYOUS CHRISTMAS TO YOU.

A MERRY CHRISTMAS & A HAPPY NEW YEAR.

For boys, there were Noah's ark figures or carts, tin or wooden soldiers, forts, tops, hoops, diabolo games, toy guns and Jacks-in-the-box.

The very rich might receive a magnificent goat-cart (Queen Victoria had one at Osborne); though this one is all too obviously a studio photographer's prop, and the little girl sitting in it, in all her Sunday finery, looks less happy than the boys with their simple coaster.

Christmas Fare

Christmas dinner is the one meal exempted from the upper-middle-class rule of calling the midday meal 'lunch' and the evening meal 'dinner'. In medieval times Christmas was celebrated with boar's head and peacock, with an occasional cygnet. The turkey arrived in the sixteenth century. The Christmas pudding originated, like the Christmas tree, in Germany – as an amorphous substance known as 'plum squash'. Gradually stiffened, it had become 'plum porridge' by Queen Anne's reign, and from this it grew into the firm sphere which appears on so many Christmas cards. An old newspaper cutting pasted on to the back of the card below, right, suggests that the custom of bathing the pudding in brandy and igniting it is 'a relic of the fire worship with which our pagan ancestors celebrated the mid-winter festival'. This seems as unlikely as another claim made in the same article, that 'The mince pie is a reminiscence of the cradle of Bethlehem and its contents were originally supposed to typify the myrrh and frankincense of the Wise Men who came from the East when the Saviour was born.' What about the gold, then? When I was in the Infants' school (1945-47) we had a Christmas dinner at school each year in which the Christmas pudding contained silver threepenny bits. Most of us took several helpings to get our hands on the money; and invariably one child swallowed a coin.

A MERRY CHRISTMAS AND A HAPPY NEW YEAR.

WISHING YOU A HAPPY XMAS.

A Merry Christmas and a Happy New Year.

MAY CHRISTMAS JOYS WITH YOU AGREE FROM CHRISTMAS WEIGHTS MAY YOU BE FREE.

Games People Played

The most popular game at children's parties was Blind Man's Buff – originally, blind man's buffet, because while the blindfolded child staggers about trying to catch somebody, the other players push him and make sport of him.

The scene within a holly and ivy border shows a game of Cat and Mouse. A 'cat' and a 'mouse' are chosen from the players. The others take hands and form a circle, into which the 'mouse' creeps, while they dance round, singing:

> *Pray Mrs Mouse are you within?*
> MOUSE *Yes, kind sir, and I'm sitting to spin.*
>
> PUSS *(outside, prowling around) Mew! mew! mew!*

The 'cat' watches his opportunity to catch the 'mouse'. He may reach her by putting his hand in the circle, provided he does not forget to mew at the same time. The mouse must try to keep in the middle of the circle, out of her enemy's reach; but she must also frequently run in and out of it, to give Puss a chance of catching her. The dancers try to help the mouse, opening and raising their arms to admit her back into the circle, and lowering their arms and drawing close together to keep out the cat.

The first card on page 40 shows a game of Forfeits. One player kneels and hides his head in the lap of another who holds up an object, asking: 'Here is a thing and a very pretty thing; what must be done by the owner of this pretty thing?' The kneeling child names a forfeit appropriate to the owner (male or female). *The Home Book* (Frederick

The Wrench Series. No. 10,111. Copyright.

.... JOLLY CHRISTMAS:" He amuses the children.

A JOYOUS CHRISTMAS AND A HAPPY NEW YEAR.

Warne, 1867) records some of the forfeits exacted in Victorian times: answering three questions without smiling; describing a rose without using the word 'and'; singing a song; kissing rabbit-wise (two children taking an end of the same piece of string in the mouth and nibbling until their lips meet); dancing with a cushion; reciting a tongue-twister; confessing whom he or she loves best in the world; or spelling Constantinople backwards.

The card below shows a game of Snapdragon: raisins covered with brandy or other spirits were set alight, and plucked out by the players while burning. The game had the spice of danger; *The Times* of 12 January 1894 reported on an accident arising from an explosion of methylated spirits used in a Snapdragon.

Apart from party games – which also included Musical Chairs, Hunt the Slipper and Charades – the children of the host family would perform their 'party pieces' on piano or violin.

A HAPPY CHRISTMASTIDE WITH PLENTY OF FUN.

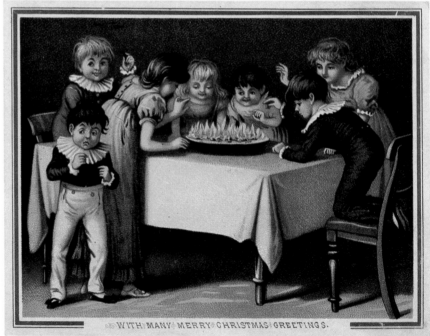

WITH MANY MERRY CHRISTMAS GREETINGS.

May loving friends surrounding make Christmas bright and gay!

E 158-1951

A YEAR OF HOPES FULFILLED BE THINE.

TO MY FRIEND — WITH LOVING GREETING.

I WISH YOU ALL THE HAPPINESS THIS MERRY TIME MAY KNOW.

CLOWN PRINTS

The English clown was the successor of the Fool or jester of medieval courts and Shakespearean plays, whom George Speaight has described as 'the safety valve of feudal society, the simpleton who could answer back to bishop and king, the fool with licence to poke fun at anyone, the instigator of coarse practical jokes'. The clown's uniform was motley or parti-coloured, often hung with bells. Speaight also astutely suggests why the custom of keeping a private fool came to an end in the seventeenth century: 'When the divine right of kings was questioned freely by parliaments there was no need for a licensed jester to remind monarchs of their humanity; the court fool was the first victim of democracy.' But the *public* fool, or clown, remained to delight patrons of the theatre, circus and fairground. The most famous clown was Joseph Grimaldi (1779-1837), whose first name was adopted for 'Joey', the clown of the Punch and Judy show – traditionally, the only one of Mr Punch's adversaries who does not get killed.

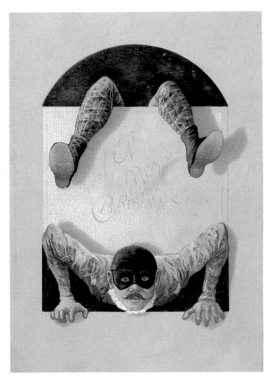

The clown figured on many Victorian Christmas cards for two main reasons: he was part of the Christmas pantomime, a favourite children's treat, and was also hired, like the conjurer, as an entertainer at children's parties in richer households; and, as many manufacturers of Christmas cards also made playing cards, their designers naturally lighted on the joker, or jester, the jolliest and most appealing character in the pack, as a suitable motif for Christmas cards.

Just stepped in to wish you a Merry Christmas.

May joys around thee brightly glow
Peace and Hope for ever flow!

Little Darlings

A special dispensation was given to children at Christmas. It was considered *their* day – the one time little boys could be seen *and* heard; though whether parental indulgence would extend to licence to rifle the jam pot (like the boy – for it is a boy – in the frilly skirts) is doubtful.

The boy in the swing, with bells, (opposite page) is by S. Hildesheimer, and on the back is a verse by Major Samuel K. Cowan, MA, who in 1884 wrote 1,005 verses for eleven firms.

F.C.P

A Merry Christmas!

The summer flowers
are faded,
Their charms no more are seen
But still the holly bloometh
With leaves of glossy green;
Its berries through each season
Still bear their crimson hue,
So will my heart for thee, dear,
Bear friendship warm and true!
.M.W.

For a happy New Year.

May you spend a merry Christmas.

S.HILDESHEIMER AND C? LIMITED.   N?1561 COPYRIGHT   PRINTED IN GERMANY

A Happy Christmas

Babes and Sucklings

Christmas was also, of course, the time when, Away in a manger, No crib for a bed, The little Lord Jesus laid down His sweet head. Crib scenes do not seem to have been as popular on nineteenth-century cards as on twentieth-century ones, in which the Kings of Orient, in head-gear like minarets, group round the manger with their expensive gifts. The babies who figure on Victorian cards are mostly comic or *kitsch* – often with verses to match.

The cupid orchestra card opposite (published by Raphael Tuck) has this verse on the back, by the Revd Frederick Langbridge, of St John's, Limerick:

'The Season's Compliments!' Ah, no!
Ah, no!
They shall not call my Season's
Greetings so.
A 'Compliment' – why that's the
formal phrase
That polished pert politeness primly
pays.
Erase the libel – write my Card above
With all the season's fond and loyal
love.

The goo-goo baby's head, perched on a pair of podgy stockinged legs, has this gem on the back, by J. H. Goring:

As pleased as a babe with a cake,
Be happy, from morning to night;
And keep all your friends wide awake
With the rattle of mirth and delight.

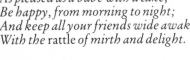

The sailor with the rockable baby on folding paper tabs also has a verse on the back. It reads:

Shiver my timbers!
  No wave on the ocean
Ere caused in his hold
  such a roll and commotion,
As this little cargo he's
  vigorously trying
To cause a small lull in
  the storm of its crying!

followed by: 'May your Christmas be free from Squalls'.

"HARK! THE HERALD ANGELS SING."

A merry Christmas and a happy New Year.

WHOLLY
HOLY

Steeped in religiosity, the Victorians were not likely to forget that Christmas was primarily a religious festival.

The 'Jerusalem' card with the round panel is dated 1872. The card with fleurs-de-lys and that with a central cross are both by Marcus Ward, of Belfast and London, who opened their London house in 1867. The firm's art director was Thomas Crane, brother of Walter. They moved to Oriel House, Farringdon Street, in 1884, a building designed by Thomas Crane.

The card bearing an angel with crossed hands has a verse on the back by R. E. Lonsdale, expressing the not very cheery hope –

And may we die, when death shall come,

On Christmas in the morning . . .

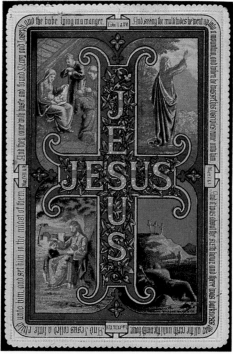

We have seen his Star in the East

GLORY TO GOD IN THE HIGHEST AND ON EARTH PEACE GOOD WILL TOWARD MEN ✠ XC·NG · CHRISTMAS GREETING

COME WITH DEVOTION AND WORSHIP THE LORD

LISTEN WHILE TO YOU IS TOLD
A TALE STILL NEW, ALTHOUGH SO OLD.

Compliments of the Season.

Crosses to Bear

MAY THE NEW YEAR BE HAPPY AND PROSPEROUS.

Though Christmas was a celebration of Christ's birth, several cards also gave a reminder of His death. Considering what the cross represented in horrible suffering, what could be more absurd and tasteless than those whimsically decorated crosses: one covered with snow and icicles (hardly likely in the Holy Land); and several festooned with flowers. Another had a pop-up cherub worked by a paper lever, which also revealed the message 'Happy New Year'. The most outlandish of all is that with a perching blue tit and a spray of fuchsia – the most popular of all flowers on Victorian cards (see p. 91).

The card with the white tassel (which when pulled reveals the legend 'Only to the cross of Jesus will I cling') is dated 1877.

O Come All Ye Fidos

Wishing you a very happy Christmas.

Dogs were the favourite animal for Christmas cards. Often, as here, they were given anthropomorphic postures – playing badminton, rocking a baby's cradle, pushing a cart, posting a letter, or wearing funny hats (see frontispiece). With all the Victorians' talent for terrible puns, none of them seems to have designed a canine Crib scene – a dog in the manger.

'E.E.G.' who wrote the verse on a delightful card showing a dog playing the flute was E. E. Griffin, who also wrote the verse on an elaborate mechanical card of a three-dimensional cradle, in the late Queen Mary's collection, and the verse on the 'black boys' card on p. 68.

With best wishes for a happy New Year

Christmas Greeting
with dearest love.

A merry Christmas.

More dogs and Doggerel

The dog saying how-d'ye-do to the crab belongs to a rich seam of *kitsch* humour which persists today in some popular newspapers – the 'unlikely friendship' theme. Cats parlay-vooing with budgerigars belong to the same genre. Helen Marion Burnside, ever ready with the right sentiment, contributes the verse on the back of this Raphael Tuck card:

*Good Morning, little Mr Crab –
Let's have a game of play,
But if you please, you mustn't
squeeze,
Because it's New Year's Day.*

The lace-edged card is dated 1869 and bears the embossed mark of Joseph Mansell of Red Lion Square, London, who published valentine-type and visiting-card-type Christmas cards from the 1860s. We also encounter a German publisher not previously illustrated: the boy with the umbrella is by Bernhard Ollendorff, who produced fine chromolithographs in Berlin from the 1870s to the 1890s. The 'crab' card was designed by Helena Maguire, who worked for Hildesheimer & Faulkner (1880-81), for S. Hildesheimer (1881, when she won two £20 prizes in their competition) and for Tuck (1886-90). Animals and birds were her speciality.

IMPUDENCE BECOMES UNBEARABLE.

A PEACEFUL AND HAPPY CHRISTMAS

A PROSPEROUS NEW YEAR.

A HAPPY NEW YEAR.

A peaceful a happy Christmas.

KITSCH CATS

With just one word I greet you here
To wish you all a Glad New Year!

A Bright and Happy Christmas.

Cats came second to dogs in popularity. They brought out the worst in Victorian artists, who set them in arch and twee poses of every kind. The sentiment-writers also enjoyed themselves. 'May you never be rubbed the wrong way' must rank as a classic among unconventional Christmas greetings. On the back of this 1880s card is a verse by S. Herbert:

They pinch our fluffy ears
*   And pull our fur,*
Then say we must not scratch
*   And bid us purr!*
'Tis hard that kittens should be
*   treated so!*
*   Such keen injustice may you never*
*   know.*

The cat in the riding-boot is no doubt pussyfooting. The one on the yacht might be happier on a catamaran.

"May you never be rubbed the wrong way."

A New Year full of brightness be yours

A Happy New Year

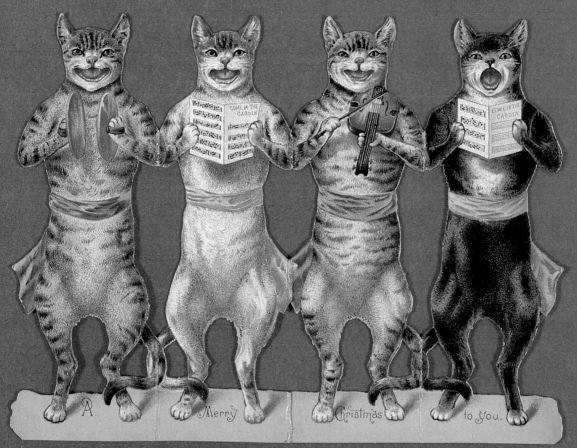

A Merry Christmas to You.

Animal Crackers

A MERRY CHRISTMAS & A HAPPY NEW YEAR

With the Season's Greetings

A Merry Christmas TO YOU.

Other animals also appeared in the Christmas menagerie. Delightful monkeys toasted the New Year with German rummers on a Hagelberg card (right); equally winsome and winning monkeys clambered over an artist's palette on a Hildesheimer & Faulkner one (above). The donkey card was probably sent from one public schoolboy to another, as it is inscribed on the back: 'The fear of C House with the love of the Lion of B House' – very Talbot Baines Reed.

The guinea-pig card (which perhaps accompanied a guinea for little Gerald who received it) was published by Ernest Nister & Co. of 24 St Bride Street, London, who were sometimes referred to as 'Nister of Nuremberg' because of their Bavarian lithography factories – the largest in Germany in the 1890s. In 1897 Nister started a new enterprise, 'Keramic printing' in colours. They issued hundreds of thousands of plates bearing a portrait of Queen Victoria.

Your Health!
May the New Year bring You
health and Wealth
And all prosperity!

Happy

may your New Year be.

Batmen and Women

A HAPPY CHRISTMAS!

"Thy thoughts I cleave to."

Bats were almost as popular on Victorian cards as belfries and bells. They were to be one of the favourite subjects of Art Nouveau designers, though their basic structure is more Gothic in feeling. Maurice Rheims, who illustrates a gold goblet decorated with a spreadeagled bat in his *L'Objet 1900* (1964), writes: 'Ces animaux, chargés de bien de crimes, ont fait en tout temps l'objet de légendes et d'illustrations terrifiantes.' But it was not until the nineteenth century that stories of the vampire bats of the South American forests reached Europe, giving the little blind flying mouse a reputation for sinister perversity most satisfying to the decadents: 'Holy Roman Vampire', Wilde suggested. The younger Strauss's comic opera *Die Fledermaus* was first performed in 1874.

Batcards ranged from the jollity of these cherub jockeys to the near-lubriciousness of Emily Thomson's design above, with its disingenuous caption, 'Thy thoughts I cleave to'.

WE COME TO WISH YOU ALL A BRIGHT NEW YEAR

Jumping for JOY

Clammy, unmelodious creatures in real life, frogs were portrayed by the card designers as frolicsome little jokers – jumping about, guzzling wine, or sitting, satiated, on water-lily leaves. They anticipate the charm of Beatrix Potter's Mr Jeremy Fisher.

The card showing the game which seems to be half-way between football and leap-frog opens out to reveal an appropriate verse by Major S. K. Cowan, MA:

May you make a hale and hearty
And contented Christmas party!
And, the New Year thro',
Care (that croaker!) may you never
Meet, but may Good Fortune, ever
Toad-y after you!

One begins to wonder in what subject Major Cowan obtained his MA. Not, it is safe to assume, English literature.

EASY ∗ LIKE ∗ THE ∗ WIND ∗ HARD ∗ TO ∗ FIND ∗ FRIENDS ∗ ARE ∗ FAITHFUL ∗ WORDS ∗ ARE

A Merry Christmas & A Happy New Year

Drink deep of
mirth this merry time!

Your heaviest care as
foam be light,
And all your days be rosy
bright.

A Merry
Family

...mas

Kindest Wishes for Christmas

WINGS AND STINGS

The insects chosen for Christmas cards were seldom of the creepy-crawly kind. Brilliant butterflies, dazzling dragonflies and the useful bee were common subjects, again happy reminders in winter of the sunnier days ahead. As one of the cards maladroitly put its,

Butterflies among the grass
Tell us time doth quickly pass

The two bee cards show a literal and grotesque metaphorical treatment of the same rather delicate subject, cross-pollination. That with the miniature cauldrons is embossed with the publisher's name – BLACKETT, NEW ST.

The larger of the two dragonfly cards is in the Art Nouveau taste, c.1905, with a strong Celtic flavour. The dragonfly (French: *libellule*) was *the* Art Nouveau insect, with wings like Tiffany stained glass – a favourite subject of Art Nouveau jewellers such as Lalique and Vever, and later in Lalique's misty blue glass.

CHRISTMAS GREETING.

Oh may thy Christmas happy be,
And naught but joy appear,
Is now the wish I send to thee,
And all I love most dear.

Copyright.

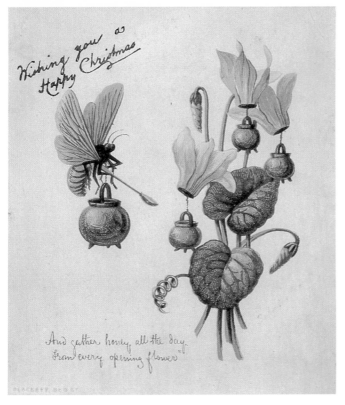

Wishing you a
Happy Christmas

"And gather honey, all the day,
From every opening flower"

A CHRISTMAS WISH.

Purer and
fairer be the flowers
Which blossom on the way,
Brighter and happier be the hours
Which mark each
Christmas Day!

Copyright.

Full Fathom Five

Slimy things from the deep were mainly ignored in subaqueous compositions of this kind. Corals, pearls and pretty shells make an attractive border; but here the verse, about frozen ground, skeleton trees and crackling dry logs, was evidently taken from stock, as it has no connexion with the sea.

The card relates to the framed compositions in dried seaweed which stood on Victorian mantelshelves – one bears this more suitable rhyme:

Call us not weeds, we are flowers of
  the sea,
For lovely and bright and gay-tinted
  are we
And quite independent of sunshine
  and showers;
Then call us not weeds, we are
  Ocean's gay flowers.

Not nursed like the plants of a
  summer parterre,
Where gales are but sighs of an
  evening air,
Exquisite, fragile and delicate flowers
Are nursed by the Ocean and rocked
  by the storms.

One Christmas card publisher, T. McGann of Gortaclare, Burren, Co. Clare, introduced in the 1880s 'what he terms a novelty in Christmas, etc. cards on which are mounted seaweeds, collected on the coasts of the localities referred to . . . The specimens certainly have a very fresh and bewitching appearance . . . they appeal directly for a hearty reception to persons of refined and cultivated tastes . . .' (*Stationer, Printer etc.* 6 September 1884.)

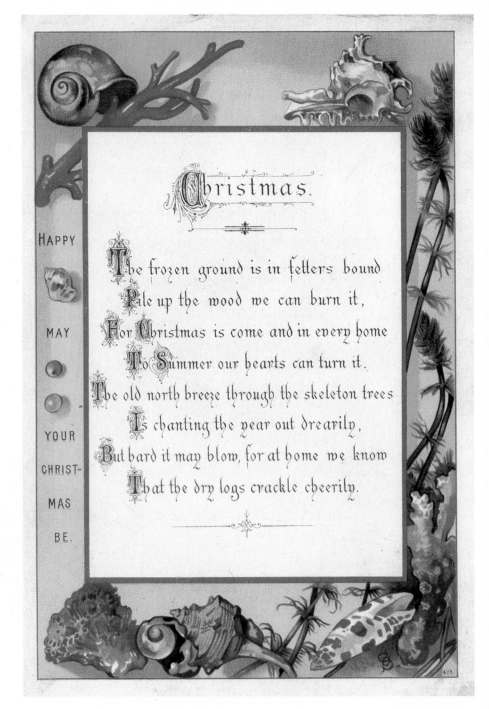

HAPPY

MAY

YOUR

CHRIST-

MAS

BE.

Christmas.

The frozen ground is in fetters bound
Pile up the wood we can burn it,
For Christmas is come and in every home
To Summer our hearts can turn it.
The old north breeze through the skeleton trees
Is chanting the year out drearily,
But hard it may blow, for at home we know
That the dry logs crackle cheerily.

Feathered Friends

This was the age of Gilbert and Sullivan's Tit Willow and Tennyson's

Birdie, rest a little longer,
Till the little wings are stronger.

Robin redbreast, then as now, was one of the most popular of all motifs; but all kinds of birds, from the homely to the exotic, flutter across Victorian cards.

The leader of the school of artists which 'humanized' birds was Henry Stacy Marks RA, a member of the St John's Wood Clique which included W. F. Yeames, the painter of 'And When Did You Last See Your Father?'. Marks also designed the frieze round the dome of the Royal Albert Hall, London. He used to go to the Zoo to draw rare birds. He produced a celebrated set of Christmas cards for Marcus Ward in 1873, but these did not have bird subjects. (Yeames and G. D. Leslie – another of the Clique – also designed fine Christmas cards.) Three Christmas-card artists who specialized in birds very much in the Stacy Marks manner were A. West, who signed the Hildesheimer & Faulkner schoolroom scene, Brighurst Lawrence (who designed and initialled the storks shown on p. 67 for S. Hildesheimer), and Alfred Crowquill.

THE COMPLIMENTS OF THE SEASON

May Christmas Day be a joyful one.

With best wishes for a happy Christmas.

Peace within
thy heart be caged
As a bird of price:
Strife nor conflict e'er
be waged
In that paradise!

A HAPPY CHRISTMAS.

A happy Christmas with unclouded sky,
We come to wish you — my duck and I.

· A MERRY CHRISTMAS AND A HAPPY NEW YEAR ·

A Hearty Christmas Greeting.

S. Hildesheimer & Co.

CHRISTMAS.

As merrily chime the bells,

To tell us "Christ is born",

So brilliantly and joyously,

May break thy Christmas morn,

And when the Bells once more proclaim,

Another year's new birth,

May every happiness attend,

Thy pilgrimage on earth.

Black Comedy

The Victorian attitude to black people would now be considered 'racist', and rightly so. But while it was patronizing, the attitude was not unfriendly. The 'nigger minstrels' to be seen at most English seaside resorts were white men 'blacked up' with burnt cork; a real black man was a sight unusual enough to seem comic. The black men and boys are nearly always portrayed smiling or laughing.

They invariably talked in pidgin English; the negro fiddler card, opposite, has this rhyme on the back:

Now dis merry season's come,
*   Hear my fiddle, tum, tum, tum,*
Join de dance while I do play
*   An' be happy while you may!*
I gib you all I hab to gib,
*   My good wishes while I lib,*
May you nebber sorrow know
*   While dis nigger draws de bow!*

And the Raphael Tuck card of Pompey and his charge on page 70 has this verse on the back:

Today, when cards and letters
*   Are pouring hourly in,*
Permit me, like my betters,
*   To make a bow, and grin.*
Now don't get mad and blindly
*   Cry, 'Take this rubbish back!'*
I really mean most kindly –
*   Although I look so black!*

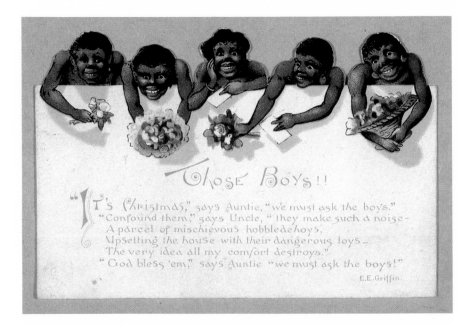

Those Boys!!

"It's Christmas," says Auntie, "we must ask the boys."
"Confound them," says Uncle, "they make such a noise—
A parcel of mischievous hobbledehoys,
Upsetting the house with their dangerous toys—
The very idea all my comfort destroys."
"God bless 'em," says Auntie "we must ask the boys!"

E.E. Griffin

A joyful Christmas to you.

A JOYOUS CHRISTMAS

A JOYOUS CHRISTMAS

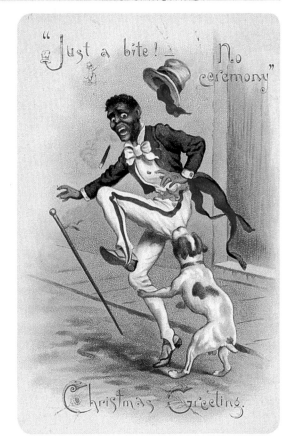

A · HAPPY · NEW · YEAR.

POMPEY · DIS · LICKLE · CARD · HAB · SENT
WID · KIND · REGARD · AND · COMPLIMENTS.

The First Golliwog

The golliwog (which so unfortunately includes the offensive 'wog') is another example of the patronizing Victorian attitude to black people; though it might be argued that snuggling up to friendly black dolls promoted, rather than hindered, racial harmony.

Like the teddy bear (named after President Teddy Roosevelt), the golliwog has an American pedigree. The artist who first drew golliwogs (or, as she spelt it, golliwoggs) to illustrate the stories her mother wrote was Florence Upton, born in New York in 1873 (though her parents were English and she returned to England). The drawings were based on a black doll Florence was given in America when she was five. Some people thought Florence's golliwogg was 'a hideous creature', but as Florence told her close American friends the Misses Martin: 'Children are way ahead in reading character: they see his beautiful character.' A golly with black seal-fur hair was marketed. Florence's book publishers, Longmans, Green & Co., gave permission for Raphael Tuck to make Golliwogg Christmas cards.

She died in 1922. On the day of her funeral miniature golliwoggs were sold in the London streets for charity, and more golliwoggs appear on her tombstone in Hampstead cemetery. The original Golliwogg ended up at Chequers, the perpetual home of the English Prime Ministers, where he remains.

"GOLLIWOGG" HARPOONS A SEAL.

To wish you A Merry New Year

By Permission of Messrs. Longmans, Green & Co.

Florence K. Upton

"GOLLIWOGG" IN FANCY DRESS.

By Permission of Messrs. Longmans, Green & Co.

Wishing you A Happy Christmas

Florence K. Upton

JOKE CARDS

Christmas was a time for fun and games, riddles and jokes. Here are five examples of Victorian humour.

The chessmen card is by 'H.H. & Co', London, who besides the 'Unique' series of which this is one, produced cards with French texts. 'J.B.B. & Co', who issued the card of the jumping boy, were better known for bird cards, including some mawkish ones of 'Silent Songsters' (dead birds) by Henry (Harry) Bright. The 'innoculation' card is by Angus Thomas of Jewin Street, London (1880s) and Silk Street (1890s), publishers of innumerable comic and novelty cards, and perpetrators of awful puns such as 'Good (four) tunes' – accompanied by four tiny manuscripts of popular songs attached to the card. Some of their cards are interesting to the political historian, for they tended to exploit topical situations, as in a card which referred to the Trafalgar Square demonstrations of 1887 (see p. 15). The 'innoculation' card probably also dates from the late 1880s.

A Merry Christmas

A MERRY CHRISTMAS TO YOU

A HAPPY NEW YEAR

AND A HAPPY NEW YEAR.

May You be **Well Innoculated**
with All the Joys of Christmas,
and have many **Successful Operations**
in The New Year.

Keep Off the Grass!

A BADGE—to wear upon Your Sleeve,
A NOTICE—" PLEASE DON'T TOUCH
MY ARM "—'tis such A TENDER SPOT,
And HURTS so very much!
That's why—if you've but just been "DONE"—
Like me—you're FEELING BLUE,
But we'll yet find consolation
In "DOING" OTHERS too.

ANGUS THOMAS, LONDON   COPYRIGHT NO. 886

ON PARADE

MAY CHRISTMAS BE HAPPY AND JOYFUL TO YOU

My Wish

Imperial pride, or jingoism, is revealed in the many cards of soldiers (sometimes, animals dressed as soldiers). The card of Highlanders has this verse on the back, by Coombes Davies, who worked for Davidson in the 1880s and 1890s:

Lads of the plaid and kilt, all hail!
Britain greets you on this day.
*   May old Christmas never fail*
To find you hearty, brisk and gay,
*   And may you all its pleasures share*
With comrades true, and lasses fair!

The card of the three martial dogs opens out to display these lines:

Like brave and well-taught soldiers,
*   The word of command we obey,*
And our orders are to wish you
*   A happy Christmas Day.*

A Merry Christmas To You.

CHRISTMAS GREETING WITH LOVE

A Happy Christmas.

Officer 16th Lancers

A happy and prosperous New Year.

Wee Folk

The world of Faery had been popularized by Richard Dadd, the artist
who went mad and killed his father;
and by Dicky Doyle, who may also
have had an insane streak.

De La Rue produced a series of
wee folk disporting themselves under
cowslip blossoms and on cactuses,
drawn with a miniaturist's skill. But
as usual the Victorian sadism was
never far away – as in the malicious
elves pelting a goose with oranges, or
the little dear who is trying to snare a
boatload of terrified pixies in her
shrimping net.

One of the grisliest Victorian cards
is of fairy bellringers (Hagelberg,
dated 1890) with a verse on the back
by E. E. Griffin, beginning:

Hark, what melodies are ringing
While the fairy bell is swinging!
Moved by dainty spirits bright,
All for your own pure delight …

May Christmas be bright with every blessing

Too, too utterly

A MERRY KISS-MAS TOO 'OO!

WISH-ING YOU A TOO TOO MERRY CHRIST MAS

The Aesthetic Movement influenced Christmas cards, together with the other decorative arts, in the 1880s. The style was mainly inspired by Japanese art, especially by wood-block prints by Hokusai, Utamaro and other Japanese masters, after the opening up of Japan to the West by Commander Perry's landing in 1867. But mixed into the style were medieval touches from Pre-Raphaelitism, and the 'five o'clock tea antiquity' popularized by the paintings of Sir Lawrence Alma-Tadema. Fans, blue china and sunflowers were the rage.

Oscar Wilde and the other apostles of Aestheticism were satirized by W. S. Gilbert in *Patience* as 'greenery-yallery, Grosvenor Gallery' and in *Punch* in the person of the drooping Mr Postlethwaite. In Christmas cards, the style was sent up by A. Ludovici, who showed in one an effeminate male adoring a sunflower in ecstasy, and by Alfred Gray, whose cards wished the recipient 'A Most Supremely Utter Christmas' and an 'Un-utterably Utter New Year'.

NEW HOPES, NEW JOYS, NEW FRIENDS SINCERE, BE THINE, DEAR FRIEND, THIS FAIR NEW YEAR.

Compliments of the Season.

Proverbs in Porcelain

Davenport Ware.

With best Christmas wishes.

Limoges China.

A Happy Christmas.

'Blue china' was one of the objects of the Aesthetes' devotion. Oscar Wilde said he hoped he could live up to his blue china; and *Punch* showed a gormless young couple wondering whether they could possibly live up to their teapot. 'Blue china' meant wares from China, decorated in under-glazed blue. Andrew Lang wrote:

*There's a joy without canker or cark;
There's a pleasure eternally new;
'Tis to gaze on the glaze and the mark
Of china that's ancient and blue.
Unchipp'd all the centuries through
It has passed since the chime of it rang,
And they fashioned it, figure and hue,
In the reign of the Emperor Hwang.*

But the fashion for china-collecting extended to English and Continental wares, too, and two of these cards show Davenport and Limoges china respectively. The Aesthetes rather liked their china to be chipped or broken: it lent comparatively modern pieces an aura of romantic antiquity.

For Auld Lang Syne!

Happiness and mirth be thine at Christmas!

Fringe Benefits

Aestheticism in excelsis! Most of the trappings of the movement are here: peacock feathers, blue china, Chinese bronze, Japanesey branch touched with snow; pallid full moon; medieval (or mock) Gothic tower. The design on the back (right), in monochrome, is in the same style, but more elegant and restrained. The olive-coloured fringe reminds us that we are still in Victorian England. So do the Mary and Joseph dish and the biblical greeting just visible on the chest-of-drawers: 'Joy and Gladness and Cheerful Feasts' (*Acts*, viii, 19).

Captivating Kate

Kate Greenaway, who belongs to the Aesthetic Movement by date, inclination and style, revived the Regency period, as Alma-Tadema revived Greek and Roman antiquity and the Pre-Raphaelites revived the Middle Ages. Though she may not be the greatest artist who turned her talents to Christmas card design, she is certainly the most sought-after by collectors.

She was born in London in 1846, daughter of a well-known engraver for the *Illustrated London News.* (She was also a cousin of Richard Dadd, of fairyland and patricide fame.) Even while at her first school in Clerkenwell she began designing Christmas cards and valentines for publishers such as Kronheim & Co. (1870-71). Later she worked for Marcus Ward and Goodall. Her work had a charming innocence, particularly appealing to John Ruskin, who in 1883 delivered an Oxford lecture on her work, 'Fairyland', and who wrote to her, after receiving her Christmas card in 1880, 'Luck go with you, pretty lass . . . To my mind it is a greater thing than Raphael's St Cecilia.'

Kate Greenaway did not sign her designs, so they can only be identified by comparison with her work in her enormously successful picture books, which brought in a fashion for 'Kate Greenaway' dresses for small girls. She died in Hampstead in 1901.

MAY CHRISTMAS BRING YOU STORE OF BLISSES
LUCKY HITS AND PRETTY MISSES.

MARCUS WARD & CO.

RAPHAEL TUCK & SONS.   WISHING YOU A HAPPY CHRISTMAS!   PRIZE DESIGN   LONDON.

RAPHAEL TUCK & SONS. ALL CHRISTMASTIDE MAY JOY ABIDE! PRIZE DESIGN LONDON.

Nymph Mania

Kate Greenaway's work inspired a host of imitators. Some were blatant plagiarists, who remained anonymous. Others were just admirers, and signed their designs: these included Jane Dealy and Eleanor Manly, both of whom designed for Hildesheimer & Faulkner. The Jane Dealy design shown here (right) is probably one of her two prize-winning designs in the H. & F. competition of 1881.

William Stephen Coleman also drew little girls (see page 11), but usually in the nude. The titles of his Christmas cards speak for themselves: 'Girlish beauties', 'Jocund Youth', 'Girlish Delights', 'Dancing Girls', 'The Bathers', 'Youthful Studies', 'Swimming Figures' and 'Nymphs of the Grove'. He was born in Horsham, Sussex, in 1829, a doctor's son. A keen naturalist, he illustrated natural history books; and when plants appear on his cards, they are usually identifiable and accurately drawn. In later life he designed more naked girls for Minton's Art Pottery Studio. He died in St John's Wood, London, in 1904.

pop-up

A large variety of mechanical, trick, pop-up or '3-D' cards was made. Some worked by pushing or pulling levers, others by pulling tassels or strings.

S. Hildesheimer of Germany specialized in fold-out cards. One, dating from 1880, had an old manor house on the outside; inside, as on a medieval altar triptych, were three Victorian versions of 'ye olde Christmasse'. Hildesheimer also produced the exquisite pop-up card shown above, which works on the same principle as children's pop-up story books of the time. On the outside is a Kate Greenaway-type small girl; the card opens to reveal a wonderful Regency garden party in progress, complete with a captive balloon ready for take-off.

Flowery Greetings

A MERRY CHRISTMAS

DINNA FORGET 1897.

May your Christmas happy be: very many may you see!

The Victorians were very keen on the Language of Flowers. A fan-shaped card of about 1870 gave a key to some of the flowers' significance: convolvulus for humility; forget-me-not for true joy; pansy for thought; bluebell for constancy; cowslip for winning grace; China aster for mutual love.

Tony Venison, in an article on the flowers used on Victorian Christmas cards in *Amateur Gardening*, 23 December 1972, described how Victorian taste in flowers changed:

The flower beds were filled with a great variety of blooms; early in Victoria's reign they would have been formally bedded out with tender pelargoniums, heliotropes, fuchsias, cannas and similar summer subjects brought from greenhouses, replaced during winter and spring by wallflowers, forget-me-nots and bulbs. But as the Queen's reign lengthened, new views on garden design came to the fore; formal bedding was banished under attacks from such critics as William Robinson and Gertrude Jekyll. To replace it there was a great swing back to growing the old-fashioned cottage garden flowers... hardy and perennial, they became subjects of endless, sweetly sentimental verses, paintings and decorations.

The English vied with the French in raising the best varieties of violets – Parma, Czar, Governor Herrick and Prince of Wales among them. Roses (including Bourbon, centifolias, damask and moss roses) were in favour; so were peonies, lilies (Madonna, tiger, or the *hemerocallis* – day lilies) which were unexciting in their colour range compared to today's varieties. Miss Jekyll popularized hollyhocks, marigolds, clarkias, larkspurs and love-in-a-mist, including the soft blue 'Miss Jekyll'. And at Christmas, of course, there were Christmas roses, *Helleborus niger*.

Compliments of the Season.

Simple daisies I have sent thee,
But they have a golden eye,
And they ever look to Heaven
Even 'neath a wintry sky.

Copyright.

BLOSSOMING TALENT

These two superbly decorative cards by Thomas Crane, art designer of Marcus Ward, mark a transitional stage between the Aesthetic Movement and Art Nouveau, the style in which Thomas's brother Walter is regarded as a leading pioneer. Already there is a move away from naturalism to stylization; the irises might be part of a Mucha poster for Sarah Bernhardt.

FAD FOR FUCHSIA

Surprisingly, the most popular flower for Christmas card designs was fuchsia. It was named after the Tübingen professor Leonhard Fuchs (1501-66) whose *Historia Stirpium* (1542) was the most organized and accurate natural history book and herbal of its time. As Hallam said, Fuchs 'secured a verdant immortality'.

The *Encyclopaedia Britannica* (1963 edition) gives this almost poetical description of the shrub:

A genus of plants of the family Onagraceae, characterized by entire, usually opposite leaves, pendant flowers, a funnel-shaped, brightly coloured, quadripartite, deciduous calyx, four petals, alternating with the calycine segments, eight, rarely ten, exserted stamens, a long filiform style, an inferior ovary and fruit, a fleshy ovoid much seeded berry.

The plant, a native of Central and South America, grew in rain forests or damp, shady and mountainous sites. It ranged from dwarf shrubs to tree-like growths. *Fuchsia Coccinea*, scarlet fuchsia, was introduced to the royal gardens at Kew in the year 1788. (That was the year George III went mad and talked to a tree; possibly he had words with a fuchsia too.) Outdoor fuchsias were usually varieties of *Fuchsia Magellanica*.

Fuchsia appears in this lush description of an archetypal Victorian garden in G. J. Whyte-Melville's novel of 1861, *Good for Nothing*:

The scarlet geraniums in the flower-garden surfeited the eye with their bright masses loading the shaven sward; the tall hollyhocks reared

their gaudy rosettes above a splendid confusion of verbena, petunia, anemone, and calceolaria spangled with spots of gold. The pendant fuchsias drooped in their last loveliness and the sweet heliotrope exhaled her dying fragrance ere she sank to decay. Only the roses were past. All was left that could extort admiration, but the balmy scent which gives its dearest charm to the summer garden was gone with the summer prime. So it is with life . . .

FIN DE SIECLE

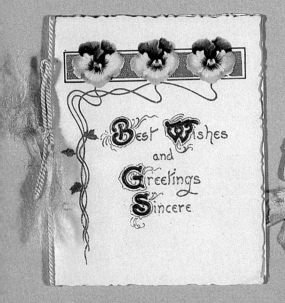

The first great flowering of Art Nouveau was in the 1890s; but it was not until after the turn of the century that the style with its 'whiplash' line (perfectly exemplified by the pansy stems and water-lily leaves here) percolated into popular taste. These embossed floral cards are nearly all by Raphael Tuck. Helen Marion Burnside was still churning out her cloying sentiments, one of which appears inside the 'petal' card with the simple word 'Greetings' on the front.

Happy hopes
and
Joyous memories

Greetings

With
Best wishes
for a happy
Christmas

Best
Wishes

Advent of The Postcard

and Postcards of the Advent

The Raphael Tuck Art Nouveau flower cards (see previous page) were already overblown and disagreeably commercialized. In the period from 1900 to the Great War, Christmas card design went into a steep decline. The postcard was now the favourite vehicle for greetings. Some have a period, 'bygone' appeal, such as these of the 'Old Crock' car and the toy zeppelin; but others just express Edwardian *faux bonhomie* and the spirit of music-hall ta-ra-ra-boom-de-ay. Davidson Brothers were responsible both for the vintage car loaded with robins and holly, and the insufferably pretty-pretty galleon with a cargo of forget-me-not and lily-of-the-valley. And this was the firm which, as recently as 1894, Gleeson White had described as having 'excellent taste'!

A BRIGHT AND HAPPY XMAS

WISHING YOU A MERRY CHRISTMAS.

JOLLY CHRISTMAS:"

His presents are not appreciated.

The Wrench Series. No. 10,103. Copyright.

A HAPPY CHRISTMAS BE THINE

After all is said and done
'Tis the finest form of fun
And a little game that you
Can prove "the nicest
game for two."